HISTORY AND FAITH

THE STORY OF THE PASSION

C. K. BARRETT

BRITISH BROADCASTING CORPORATION

Published by the
British Broadcasting Corporation
35 Marylebone High Street
London, W.1.

First published 1967
© *C. K. Barrett 1967*

Printed in England by Brown Knight & Truscott Ltd, London and Tonbridge

No. 7152

CONTENTS

I   WHAT HAPPENED   5

II   THE SETTING   11

III   FEAST AND FAST   17

IV   THE SERVANT OF THE LORD   23

V   THE SON OF MAN   29

VI   CONCLUSION   35

I. WHAT HAPPENED

Most of the Holy Week addresses I have heard have been 'devotional'; that is, they have presented Jesus Christ, crucified and risen, in such a way as to make a direct appeal to the hearer's mind, imagination, feeling, and will. They have said, in effect, 'He died for you; what response do you intend to make?' There is nothing wrong in addresses of this kind. I have given them myself, and hope to do so again; but not this week. At least, I mean to start in a different way; not with devotion, but with history.

Why not? Everyone, whether he is a Christian or not, would agree that the crucifixion and resurrection of Jesus are at the heart of Christianity. But the crucifixion and resurrection were not ideas that someone invented out of his own head; they were events that happened. This is clear enough about the crucifixion, but it is true of the resurrection too, for even if you are not prepared to accept the New Testament stories of the appearances of Jesus and the empty tomb, you will recognize at least that something happened which caused the disciples of Jesus to believe that though he had been dead he had now come to life; and this is enough history to begin with. When Paul sums up his preaching in the words (1 Corinthians 15.3), Christ died for our sins, and was buried, and on the third day he was raised from the dead, he is not talking theology (though he was ready enough to go on to talk theology – and so should we be), but history.

This history – as real as the Battle of Hastings or the war in South East Asia – is the foundation of our faith; it cannot be wrong to begin by looking at it, and talking about it, as history. It is, perhaps, not as simple as it seems.

Jesus was crucified. Who crucified him? For centuries the church answered, The Jews crucified him; and in that belief Christians have, from time to time, committed crimes against the Jewish people of which Christians today ought to be – and, I believe, are – ashamed. The record is a sorry one, and nothing can excuse it. Jesus himself did not encourage us to take vengeance: If anyone strikes you on one cheek, let him have the other one too (Matthew 5.39). Even if it had ever been right to take vengeance, there was little to be gained by exacting it from later generations who could have had nothing to do with the crucifixion. Anti-Judaism is inexcusable, even if the old charge against the Jews is right. But is it?

Jesus was crucified. But no Jew ever crucified anyone. It was not a Jewish punishment. If you heard that a criminal had been executed in the electric chair you would know for certain that he had not been condemned by a British court and executed here. We have never used the electric chair. The Jews never used crucifixion. You can read in the Mishnah (a very old collection of Jewish laws): 'The Court had power to inflict four kinds of death penalty: stoning, burning, beheading, and strangling' (Sanhedrin 7.1). Crucifixion is not among them; it was a Roman penalty, inflicted on slaves, and on rebels against the state. In the great war against Rome, about forty years after the death of Jesus, the Romans crucified many of the prisoners they took: 'so great was their number, that space could not be found for the crosses, nor crosses for the bodies' (Josephus, *Jewish War* v,451).

We are running into difficulties here. Should we conclude, from the fact that he was crucified, that Jesus must have led an armed revolt against Rome? Some people have said something of the kind, and drawn up quite elaborate – and quite imaginary – stories of how it happened. But when you put them beside the teaching of Jesus they do not make sense – though it is certainly possible that he may have been confused with a rebel. He was executed as the 'King of the Jews' (Mark 15.26), and one at least of his followers was ready to use a sword in Gethsemane. The fact remains, however, that the preacher of the Sermon on the Mount and the foiled revolutionary do not look like the same person.

Suppose then we come back to the Jews. After all, Paul himself says (1 Thessalonians 2.15) that the Jews killed the Lord Jesus; and only a few years before he wrote those words he himself had been persecuting Christians as the agent of the Council that had examined Jesus' case. Paul should have known; and this is what he says. When, however, we turn to the gospel accounts of the 'trial' of Jesus we encounter another problem. In the course of the proceedings the High Priest asks Jesus directly, Are you the Christ, the Son of the Blessed One? Jesus answers, I am; and you shall see the Son of man sitting on the right hand of the Power, and coming with the clouds of heaven. Upon this, the High Priest tears his clothes, and says, What further need have we of testimony? You have heard the blasphemy. And the Council declared him to be liable to the death penalty (Mark 14.61-4).

Jesus then was judged guilty of blasphemy, and was therefore liable to capital punishment. But here are two more difficulties. If he was guilty of blasphemy, he should have been stoned, not crucified; the Jewish law is quite clear about this. And can he have been guilty of blasphemy? Let me quote the Mishnah (Sanhedrin 7.5) again: ' "The blasphemer" is not culpable unless he pronounces the Name itself' – that is, the name of God, of which the consonants but not the vowels are given in the Old Testament, and which no Jew (except the High Priest once a year) would ever allow himself to utter. Jesus had not used this name; he had not even used the word God, but had spoken of the Son of man sitting on the right hand of 'the Power'.

The fact is that both Romans and Jews were in a difficult position; and the more sincere their opposition to Jesus the greater the difficulty. The teaching of Jesus was completely incompatible with armed revolution – a *coup d'état* in which Jesus might hope to depose first Pontius Pilate and then the Emperor, and rule in their place. This, however, did not mean that he constituted no danger to Roman authority; he was a far greater danger than a thug with a cudgel, or a cloak-and-dagger conspirator. The trouble was, how to state the case against him, and get rid of him.

Again, the bitterest Jewish enemies of Jesus could not plausibly allege that he was a bad-tempered fellow who in a fit of rage had cursed and used the name of God. He was, however, a far greater peril to Judaism than such a blasphemer could be. A swear-word here or there is not a serious threat to any religion; but the teaching of Jesus came down to this, that not the Jewish law but he himself was the way to God. 'You have heard that it was said to the men of old . . . but I say unto you . . .' (Matthew 5.21, etc.). He could place his own authority above Moses. This was not blasphemy in the technical sense, but it undermined the authority of Judaism. So the Jews too had a problem. If the Roman court had to define sedition that was not sedition, the Jewish court had to define blasphemy that was not blasphemy.

It is not surprising then that historical analysis of the gospel stories of the trial and death of Jesus runs into difficulties. There never was a plain and simple tale to tell, and if any of the gospels offered one we should rightly suspect it of being fiction. I am not, however, going to dig further into the history now. All I mean to observe at the moment is this. Even more than most things that happen in history the death of Jesus was a complicated event, made up of mixed motives and cross-purposes. It was certainly not a transcript on the page of history of a set of ready-made theological ideas; the thing happened, and then people set to work to find out what it meant.

Turn now from the crucifixion to the resurrection. Again historical analysis runs into difficulties. In Samuel Butler's novel *The Way of all Flesh* the last straw that breaks his faith and drives Ernest Pontifex out of the church is the discovery that the resurrection stories in the four gospels cannot be harmonized into a single consistent narrative. No one is likely to be troubled by that discovery today, for what it means is that whatever it was that happened on the first Easter Day was not the sort of thing that could be written up in the form of a railway timetable. It was far too big for that; and it is not in the least surprising that various people saw it in different ways, and could not in the end agree on the order and location of all the events. All this, I think, is reasonably clear.

But what was it that happened? It is here that we meet a rather different kind of historical question. The New Testament says (Acts 3.15, etc.), God raised him from the dead.

Christians believe this to be true, but it is not the sort of statement that can be proved – or disproved – by a simple appeal to history. An appeal to history can approach it. It can show beyond any reasonable doubt that men like Peter and Paul honestly believed that they had seen Jesus alive, and that their conviction was so solid that it shaped the rest of their lives. It can show that neither Jews nor Romans ever produced the dead body of Jesus. They may never have looked for it, but if they did, they did not find it. These observations, and others like them, have their use. But they do not – and, as far as I can see, they cannot – prove that God actually did something. At least in theory, some other explanation will always be possible.

What this means is that when Christians say of Jesus, God raised him from the dead, they are expressing the belief that, at that point, something that does not belong to the ordinary course of history came into history from outside, leaving behind it the marks of a unique disturbance (which historians can study), but itself too fine to be caught in their fishing nets.

In a different way, we come back to the observation I made about the crucifixion stories. The stories of the resurrection are not the dead product of someone's attempt to write out his theology in narrative form. They are fragmentary, unsystematic, and alive. The event came first, and it knocked everyone off balance. Then they pulled themselves together, and tried to work out what it meant.

It may be that I have given a wrong impression in some of the things I have said in this talk. When you approach the gospels as a historian it is easy – and it is not wrong – to speak of the crucifixion and resurrection as problems. But as a historian you must also recognize that this is not how the first Christians saw the crucifixion and resurrection. To them, they were not problems, but the answers to all the problems. How is a man to live in this world, where wickedness and suffering are stamped upon the lives of his fellow-men, and a rich stream of the same commodities wells up from his own consciousness? You may not agree with them, but they knew that the answer was in Jesus Christ, crucified and risen.

They knew the answer was there; but it was not worked out. The theology was not ready-made; they had to think it through. And this week I mean to trace out in outline some of the steps they took. We shall understand the New Testament message better if we can follow through some of the processes by which it reached its familiar form.

II. THE SETTING

THE FIRST Good Friday and Easter found the disciples of
Jesus equipped not with a theory but with a fact, or a group
of facts. Something had happened which had opened a new
world to them, and given to life possibilities, and a perspec-
tive, that they had not previously been aware of. The forces
of evil – sin and death – had been dealt a mortal blow, and
they themselves were now free men. Of all this they were
sure, and because they were sure of it they proceeded to
behave with an extraordinary indifference to their own
interests. But how this had come about was a different
matter, and a question to which they had no quick answer.
They were left with the task of explaining why the death
and resurrection of Jesus had been the necessary way in
which God had worked, and how this death and resurrection
had brought about the new situation in which they were
living.

This is, roughly, the point we reached at the end of
yesterday's talk. I have, perhaps, exaggerated it slightly. The
earliest disciples, in the task of explaining the crucifixion and
resurrection, did not have to start quite from scratch. There
was material in the Old Testament ready to hint at some
explanation of the saving power of righteous suffering; and
the Jesus who died was the Jesus who for some time had
lived with them and instructed them. But neither the Old
Testament nor the teaching of Jesus are likely to be helpful
if you do not understand them; and that the disciples had
not understood the crucifixion and resurrection as the working
out of an already cut and dried programme is clearly shown
by the fact that when the time came they betrayed, denied,
and forsook their Master in the most disgraceful manner. It
was only afterwards, when the resurrection had turned defeat
into victory, that they turned back to the Old Testament
and the teaching of Jesus, both of which they now saw in a
new light, to explain what had happened and the position
in which they now found themselves.

What were the first steps they took? What corresponding

steps must we take if we are to follow up the lines on which
their thought developed and so reach for ourselves an understanding of the crucifixion and resurrection? They were Jews
living in the first century; this means that we must be prepared to begin by trying to step into a world of thought
different from that in which we ourselves have grown up.
This step, let me add, is not simply a piece of antiquarianism
(though there would be nothing to be ashamed of in that);
the practical use of it, however, cannot be seen in advance,
but only as we continue with our investigation.

We know a good deal about the religion of Jews in the
time of Jesus. It was a religion based partly on the faithful
observance of a law God had given in the past, and partly
on the hope that God would do something for his people in
the future. The hope was sometimes formal, occasionally
despairing, often fervent. This way of looking at life goes
back to the Old Testament, where the prophets, and the
history writers who worked in the spirit of the prophets,
looked at things in terms of the belief that the true meaning
of a sequence of events was to be seen only when the last
event was reached. It is best to see this in particular examples.
Thus, the majority of Jews in the time of Jeremiah might
hold the view that so long as they maintained the temple
ritual they would be secure, and could therefore afford to
disobey the word of God and persecute the prophets who
spoke it. Jeremiah knew this was wrong, but there was no
way in which he could *prove* that it was wrong; only the end
of the story – the coming of the Babylonians to sack city and
temple alike – could do that, could prove that God cared
very little for temple rituals, and very much for obedience.
Again, in the next generation, when they were exiled to
Babylon, the Jews believed that God had turned his back on
them for good. 'My way is hid from the Lord, and my judge-
ment passed over from my God' (Isaiah 40.27). They were
wrong; the prophet knew that they were wrong; and knew
that the truth would come out at the end of the story, when
the ransomed of the Lord returned and came singing to Zion
(Isaiah 51.11).

This was a true insight into the meaning of history, and

there is much to learn from it. 'Have an eye to the end of things' is old and wise advice. 'The last of life, for which the first was made', is likely to make the rest intelligible, as it can hardly be if you only look at it in mid-stream. The Old Testament prophets were right – as right as they could be within the limited area which they were content to cover; but the 'ends' with which they worked were only relative ends. As soon as the historical process, of national apostasy and divine retribution, in which Jeremiah was involved, was at an end, a new process, of national despair and divine comfort, began. And so things went on. It was possible to divide history into reasonably self-contained stretches, each with a beginning, a middle, in which the truth was often buried under puzzling and misleading events, and then an end; but the end was only a partial end, and consequently could give only a partial explanation of a part of history.

In the time of Jesus the Jews were trying to go further than this. This was not simply because, intellectually, they wanted to grasp the meaning of history as a whole, but because they had come to despair of finding a solution for the world's ills within the limited framework of the human story. The Babylonian armies were not sufficient to punish the wicked, nor the Persian emperor Cyrus to vindicate the righteous. The powers of evil had gained control, and there could be only partial relief from their tyranny until, at the end of time, God should himself take back all authority into his own hands, where it belonged, destroying evil and establishing and manifesting his own royal authority. This really would be the end of this world, and it would bring the whole truth to light. It would show that sinners cannot get away with their sin for ever; that those who suffer for righteousness' sake will not lose their reward; that the Lord is king, however many things may seem to contradict his rule.

Within this framework of thought men looked and longed for the setting up of God's kingdom. One of the oldest synagogue prayers runs, 'May he set up his kingdom in your lifetime and in the lifetime of all Israel, speedily, and at a near time'. This conviction enabled them to stand fast in the dark days, for they believed that the good time to come would be preceded by a time of suffering. Things would have to get worse, much worse, before they could get better; and what was expected of God's people was that they should hold fast through the suffering, and so find their way into the glory beyond.

Now the men who wrote the gospels, and those who, before gospels were written down, passed on by word of mouth the material out of which they were made, were familiar with these ideas. For example, in the gospels you will read a great deal about the kingdom of God. Mark's first account of what Jesus had to say is given in these words: Jesus came into Galilee, proclaiming the good news of God, and saying, The time is up, the kingdom of God has come near; repent, and believe in this good news (Mark 1.14,15). To him, it was worth any price to get into the kingdom of God: If your eye gets in your way, pluck it out; it is better for you to get into the kingdom of God one-eyed, than to have two eyes and be thrown into Gehenna (Mark 9.47).

In particular, some of the parables are connected with the kingdom of God. Here is one of the shortest: How can we make a likeness for the kingdom of God? In what parable are we to put it? It is like a grain of mustard seed, which, when it is sown in the earth, is smaller than all other seeds on earth; and yet, when it is sown, it grows up and becomes bigger than all other plants, and makes big branches, so that the birds of the sky can make their nests under its shadow (Mark 4.30-32). You will remember other parables like this, especially the parable of the Sower, and the one about the farmer who, having sown his seed, leaves it to grow on its own until harvest time comes.

All these parables have the same plot. In each there are two critical moments, with a mysterious, invisible, but essential connection between them. First, there is the present. This is the time when the seed is put in the ground. It is small; much of it is wasted; it is (or appears to be) neglected; what is more, it must die. It simply rots away in the earth. But second, there is the harvest. The small seed becomes a big shrub; the seed, wastefully scattered over all kinds of land, produces, in the good ground, a yield that more than makes up for what is lost; the farmer has plenty of work to do in the end. And somehow the beginning and the end are connected, at least to the extent that if there were no beginning there would be no end. In the first century the Jews of Palestine knew little about scientific agriculture, but they did know that there was a connection between sowing and reaping, even if they could not explain it.

This is the framework within which Jesus explained his work. He proclaimed the coming of the kingdom of God. To this proclamation his opponents could have replied, Yes, we know that, when he sees fit, God will establish his kingdom; but it is absurd to suggest that anyone so insignificant, uneducated, feeble, and despised as you can have anything to do with it. To this the answer comes back: There is the same kind of connection that there is between the minute seed, rotting in the ground, and the harvest that will before long cover the countryside. Jesus' humble and obscure earthly life, culminating in a horrible and dishonourable death, was somehow organically connected with the coming of the kingdom of God in glory and power. We are familiar with the words, 'When thou hadst overcome the sharpness of death, thou didst open the kingdom of heaven to all believers'. But the connection is closer. It was in and by enduring the sharpness of death that he made the kingdom available. The suffering was the hard time which the prophets had already learned to see as coming before the good time, when evil was defeated and God triumphant.

Precisely at this point, however, we run into a difficulty, which we shall have to keep in mind and work at through the rest of this week. It is quite easy to see what the difficulty is. When men looked out of a troubled present into the blissful future they hoped for, it was not hard for them to fit suffering into the programme. The devil would have a last fling; God's people would be persecuted; but they must stick it out. Some no doubt would fail. Under pressure, they would give up their faith, and choose the easy way out. If they did, they would miss the reward. Those who had suffered, and they only, would share in the blessings of the kingdom. Glory was contingent upon steadfastness in distress. To know this

provides one very important step in understanding the crucifixion and resurrection: God's final purpose of glory and
goodness has room in it for suffering. But the story in the
gospels departs from the pattern, because in it all the suffering
falls in the end on one person only – Jesus.

The difficulty is reflected in two sets of sayings which the
gospels contain. The first speaks of suffering as the common
lot of Jesus and his disciples. He challenges them, for example,
in these words: If anyone wishes to come after me, let him
deny himself and take up his cross; that is how he must follow
me (Mark 8.34). To James and John he says, You shall
indeed drink my cup, and be baptized with the baptism I
am baptized with (Mark 10.39). The plain meaning of these
sayings seems to be: I shall suffer, and you will suffer too.
Over against them we may put this one: The Son of man
came not to be served, but to serve, and to give his life as a
ransom for many (Mark 10.45) – that is, Jesus undertakes to
give his life in the place of others, that they may go free.
Who then are to suffer? all, or one? If only one suffers, how
can that help the rest? How can he open the kingdom of
heaven for them?

We must go back to the historical fact: after the crucifixion
and resurrection of Jesus his disciples knew that this had
happened, that a new age had dawned, and was running its
course alongside the old order of sin, suffering, and death.
But how? How had Jesus' suffering and death come to affect
others? And how could they enter into what he had done,
and take their places in the kingdom of God? These questions
had still to be answered.

III. FEAST AND FAST

THE CONTEMPORARIES of Jesus began with a belief that is well summed up in the words of exhortation that Paul and Barnabas hand on to their converts: It is through many tribulations that we must enter the kingdom of God (Acts 14.22). God's people must hold out through the climax of suffering in order to share in the glory to come. This is the vital jumping-off ground for any attempt to explain the suffering of Jesus – at least, if we are to explain it genetically, and understand how the New Testament writers came to see it and interpret it as they do. God's saving purpose for his people includes suffering: this is a fixed point. It is not surprising; nor does it mean that God, in a vindictive spirit, means to knock man about a bit first, so as not to make things too easy and pleasant for him – though this is not to say that punishment and retribution have no place in the story. It is rather that suffering is the consequence of faithfulness. The world being what it is, faithfulness and obedience to God are the way to run into trouble; the way to avoid trouble is to swim with the stream and be unfaithful. It is like supporting the legal government in a state that has been taken over by some illegal regime; it is asking for trouble. Suffering, then, there will be, but if you stick it out things will come right in the end.

There are two ways in which the New Testament story of the death and resurrection of Jesus upsets this happy-ending drama. In the first place, it is not content to wait for the happy ending until it gets to the last chapter of the history book. This must not be exaggerated. The New Testament goes on saying as firmly and clearly as anyone that the book does not go on for ever, but will have a last chapter. But though it keeps the idea that only at the very end will the last enemy be overthrown, it insists that with the resurrection of Jesus the happy ending has already begun. This was the conviction with which the Christian movement began; it was a conviction and an experience. Rationalizations, some of which we shall look at, followed; but they did not begin the

process. Easter was the beginning of the end, the life of
heaven brought forward into this world, so as to rub shoulders
with the old conditions of sin, suffering, and death.

That is one way in which the New Testament story of
Jesus upsets the conventional religious expectations of the
day. The second is to be found in the area of suffering involved. In the familiar story, suffering falls upon the people
of God; some buy their way out – and so far as they have
any future at all it is one of shame and everlasting contempt;
the faithful win through their sufferings to the bliss God has
prepared for them. But in the gospels all the suffering falls
upon one person. There are some who are called to share it
with him; but they all run away, so that there is only one of
the righteous left to suffer. How could his suffering affect the
destiny of others?

Again I have begun by asking questions, setting out problems that need answers. Let me make again the point that
this does not mean that the crucifixion and resurrection presented themselves to the first Christians as a problem; they
were not a problem but a Gospel. But a Gospel means good
news, and if news is to be communicated it has to be thought
through, and we are trying to analyse the movement of early
Christian thought. We took one step by recognizing that the
first Christians were brought up in a way of looking at history
that included two stages, a stage of suffering and then a
stage of glory. We now have two further questions to pursue.

The next step is to exercise a little historical imagination.
Suppose you were a Jew of the first century. Where would
you look for answers to these questions? I think there is little
doubt that you would start with the religious institutions that
you knew; and not much doubt that this in fact happened.
In what remains of this talk I am going to deal with two
great Jewish religious institutions, both of which are used
in the New Testament in the attempt to explain the crucifixion and resurrection.

All the gospels record that Jesus was killed at or about the
time of the feast of Passover. There seems to have been an
independent recollection of the fact in Jewish circles too, for
there is an old tradition to the effect that 'on the eve of

Passover they hanged Jesus, and the herald went before him for forty days, saying, "He is going forth to be stoned, because he has practised sorcery and beguiled and led astray Israel. Let everyone who knows anything in his defence come and plead for him." But they found nothing in his defence and hanged him on the eve of Passover' (Sanhedrin 43a). This was not borrowed from Christian sources, and the knowledge behind it is imperfect; but it does underline the connection between the death of Jesus and Passover.

This general connection is, I think, all that we need at present to be concerned with. There is a difficult question of dating lurking in the background, for while three of the gospels – Matthew, Mark, and Luke – say that the Last Supper was actually a Passover meal, the fourth says that Jesus died at the time when the Passover sacrifice was offered, so that by the time the Jews in general were eating their meal he was already dead. The Last Supper came a day earlier. The whole question is further complicated by the fact, which the discovery of the Dead Sea Scrolls has emphasized, that in the first century the Jews were not in agreement about how their calendar should operate. Some of them may have celebrated Passover on a different day from others. Fortunately, for our purposes this does not matter very much. Whatever the details may have been, it was against the background of Passover that the crucifixion and resurrection happened.

Passover was a feast of deliverance. In the Old Testament its roots go back to the Exodus, when, under Moses, the people were brought out of Egypt and led safely through the Red Sea. In the time of Jesus it was primarily a commemoration of this historical event, which had been the foundation of Israel as an independent people. But it was more than a commemoration. Every Jew taking part in it was instructed to think of himself as if he personally had come out of Egypt. And deliverance was not merely brought up-to-date; it was projected into the future, in that the Passover reaffirmed the hope that God would act to deliver his people and set up his kingdom.

So when Paul speaks of Christ as *our* Passover, sacrificed

for us (1 Corinthians 5.7), the first thing he means is that the death and resurrection of Jesus are the scene and the instrument of a divine act of deliverance. Back in the Old Testament, the Exodus was something God did for a mob of slaves who were in no position to help themselves. He did it for no virtue or merit of theirs, but simply out of love, and because he had made a promise to their ancestors. If Christ is a new Passover, this means that God is, through him, fulfilling his promise and acting in love on behalf of those who cannot help themselves. In practical terms, this means that the historical event, in which the disciples, seeing the crucifixion ahead, ran fast to save their skins, and so failed their Master, is taken care of from the beginning. God is undertaking to deal with a situation in which human resources have been strained to breaking point. The question how one could suffer so as to affect the destiny of others was not the wrong question to ask, but it left something out of account; it left out the fact that God himself could step in to use the events of history as he pleased – as we know he did.

Even with this, however, we have not quite finished with the themes of Passover. Let me quote more fully what Paul has to say about this: Don't you know that a little yeast affects the whole lump of dough? Clean out the old yeast, in order that you may be a new lump of dough – as in fact you are free from yeast. For our Passover has been sacrificed – I mean, Christ. So let us keep the feast, not with old yeast, the yeast of malice and evil, but with unleavened loaves of sincerity and truth (1 Corinthians 5.6-8). It seems to me that, unless you have the clue, that must sound pretty near to nonsense. Let me explain.

In old copies of the Passover Haggadah, or service, you are likely to see on the first page a picture of an old man carrying a candle. He is looking for yeast, or, more strictly, for any kind of fermenting material. This is because the feast of Passover was bound up with the use of unleavened bread, bread made without yeast. Not only was yeast not used in the making of Passover bread, a devout Jew would, before Passover came, do a sort of spring-cleaning, to clear out of his house every bit of yeast-like or fermenting stuff. This was already in New Testament times an age-old custom, and it is not surprising that yeast had come to be a stock proverbial expression for evil; Paul himself twice quotes the proverb, A little yeast affects the whole lump. Let us get the order of events quite clear: you cleared the yeast out of your house, you sacrificed the Passover lamb, and then you celebrated the feast. That is a straightforward sequence, but the New Testament adaptation of it is more complicated, for it begins with stage two, the sacrifice. It could not really begin anywhere else, because everything begins with God's initiative in acting on behalf of those who cannot help themselves, and do not deserve that anyone else should do so. Because the sacrifice has been offered, the feast, stage three, begins. This is what Christianity is, and has been since the first Easter Day. But, to catch up with ourselves, we have to go back to stage one, and clear out the old fermenting stuff – the yeast of malice and evil, as Paul explains it. Because one has suffered, all may celebrate the feast; but before it can be celebrated in its fullness there is a process of moral spring-cleaning to carry out.

Now let me turn briefly to the other great institution of Judaism that the New Testament writers used. Passover was a feast; there was only one fast in the Jewish calendar, the Day of Atonement, when the accumulation of a year's sins, which stood between the people and their God, was set aside. This was the one day in the year when one man only, the High Priest, was allowed to enter the most holy part of the Temple. He took with him the blood of a sacrifice that had been offered in the outer courts, and by means of it made atonement for himself and for all his people.

This is another of the Old Testament pictures that Paul lightly touches on, making the same sort of adjustment that he makes when he deals with the Passover. When you look at Christ, he says, you see a way of atonement that God himself has provided; God does not wait for man's initiative. When Christ as the High Priest takes blood as the means of atonement, it is his own blood that he takes. The sacrifice he has offered is not one external to himself; it is himself. And what he does is not a mechanical wiping of the national

slate; it is something that a man can share in only by faith –
that is, by some kind of personal acceptance and participation.

I am uncomfortably aware that parts of this talk must have
seemed like mere archaeological digging in the ancient
history of religion. I shall show before the end of the week
how near home it all comes, but I should like now to underline a point I have already made. The people who had been
with Jesus, and those who joined them in the fellowship of
the Christian faith, started not from a theory but from a conviction, which they knew to be of practical significance in
their lives. But being intelligent people, and having in
addition the desire to communicate their conviction, they
had to find language in which to express it, and naturally
began in the universe of ideas that was familiar to them, and
to their neighbours. With the crucifixion and resurrection
the decisive hour had struck on the world clock. The one
who died and rose again had passed through suffering and
victory into the new world. What about the rest of them?
Let us try to explain the situation in terms of the Passover,
in terms of the Day of Atonement, and so on. It was not
their fault that all the tools they used broke in their hands;
it may be that if we try to find language of our own it too
will break down.

IV. THE SERVANT OF THE LORD

FACED WITH the crucifixion and resurrection of Jesus as facts – not as ideas – his disciples had some hard thinking to do. Their problem was not ours. When we look at the story our natural reaction is to say, But how could a dead man come to life again? Is this not so impossible as to be absolutely incredible? This was not their question. They asked, Since this has undoubtedly happened, what does it mean? We have already seen that their first step was to place the crucifixion and resurrection in what they understood to be God's programme for the restoration of the world. The story was one that must move through shame and suffering into glory. Well, it had done so; only one had taken all the shame and suffering upon himself and had passed through them into glory. Now there was the possibility that those who were prepared in some way to join in the suffering afterwards might get a share of the glory in advance – before, that is, God brought the whole human story to an end. This was exactly what they knew had happened. They were ready now to die with and for Christ; and in that readiness they had found themselves living in a new world, even while the old world still went on. But how could you put this into words so as to convey it to others?

Institutions such as Passover and the Day of Atonement helped. People knew what they meant, and they could be adapted. They spoke of an act of deliverance and of forgiveness on God's part. But there were limits to their usefulness. Consider Passover, for example. It was all very well to tell a man participating in the Passover that he must consider that it was not only his ancestors but he personally who had been delivered from bondage in Egypt. This was true enough in a way – for there is a real solidarity in the race, and it is not (for example) altogether nonsense if I say, We won the battle of Waterloo (even though none of us was about in the year 1815). But it was true only in a way. The man in question had no more been a slave in Egypt than I was a soldier in Wellington's army. Moreover, as Christians, men could see more clearly that there was an even worse slavery than bondage in Egypt, and that most of all a man needs to be delivered from bondage to himself. There was a measure of impersonality about Passover which limited its usefulness as a way of explaining what God does for men through Jesus.

As for the Day of Atonement, it was on any showing aimed at dealing with sins of ignorance. There were many laws in Judaism, and it was not hard to transgress one inadvertently; you meant no harm, you simply overlooked it. For this kind of inadvertence the Day of Atonement made provision. But this only touches the edge of man's need. What of the occasions when I know quite well what is right and what is wrong, and choose what is wrong? when I snap my fingers in God's face, and flout his commandments? Again, I need something that can only be expressed in terms of personal relationship.

That God was now dealing with men in the personal terms they needed, the people of the New Testament were convinced. But how, within the framework provided by the Old Testament and the teaching of Jesus, were they to express this?

It is not surprising that some of them turned to what is perhaps the most personal chapter in the Old Testament, the fifty-third of Isaiah. This is important, and I must remind you at least of some of the key sentences.

'He was despised, and rejected of men; a man of sorrows, and acquainted with grief: and as one from whom men hide their face he was despised and we esteemed him not.

Surely he hath borne our griefs, and carried our sorrows: yet we did esteem him stricken, smitten of God, and afflicted. But he was wounded for our transgressions, he was bruised for our iniquities: the chastisement of our peace was upon him; and with his stripes we are healed. All we like sheep have gone astray; we have turned every one to his own way; and the Lord hath laid on him the iniquity of us all.'

This is familiar; there is more in the chapter, but this will serve to remind you of the whole. But what does it mean? You may remember the New Testament story of the evangelist Philip, who found an Ethiopian traveller reading this chapter as he drove in his chariot. Do you understand what you are reading? said Philip. No, the man did not; did not even know who it was the prophet was speaking of. And when Philip answered that it was about Jesus, this was not, I suspect, anything like the answer the Ethiopian expected. But we must do some work for ourselves.

If we were to ask the Ethiopian's question – About whom was the prophet writing? – we should soon be involved in a number of technical questions to which there are no simple answers. I do not mean that they are questions that ought not to be asked, only that it is hard to get much good out of them in a short time. Let us ask a different kind of question. Is innocent suffering a problem, or the answer to a problem? It may be both. That it is a problem no one is likely to doubt. We have seen enough of it in our own age. No one can look, for example, at the pictures which appear night after night on the news bulletins of homeless and frightened children in Vietnam without asking why such little ones have to endure such horrors. But this is suffering that is not only innocent but involuntary. What of it when suffering is voluntarily accepted by an innocent person who knows what he is doing and accepts suffering as the price and means of achieving an end? if, for example, someone volunteers to go out to Vietnam to live with and work for the suffering children? There are some problems which only this kind of innocent suffering can solve.

We can now edge a little nearer to Isaiah's situation. When they were first deported to Babylon the Jews were prepared to accept that they were getting what they deserved. They had been unfaithful and disobedient, and if God chose to use Babylon as their executioner he was within his rights. But time went on. A generation and more passed by. The Jews in Babylon had taken their lesson to heart and pulled themselves together. They edited and codified their law – and, what was more, began to take it seriously and to obey it. They remembered what the prophets had said, and began to put their oracles together in written books. They developed their synagogues in which they could read and hear and study both the law and the prophets. They had learned their lesson; punishment had had its remedial effect; but punishment was still going on. Why? Why should Babylon tyrannize over men who, though far from perfect, were relatively in the right? That was the particular form in which the problem of innocent suffering impinged on them.

This was the place where the prophet began to see innocent suffering as an answer. If men were sometimes expected to suffer for their own sins, perhaps they could sometimes accept an overdose and suffer for other people's sins too, even though those other people might cause the suffering, or mock the sufferer. They would learn in the end. 'We thought God must be punishing him, we thought he was suffering on his own account; we despised him. But now we can see that he was suffering for us; that he was bearing the consequences of our sins; that his wounds mean our freedom' (Isaiah 53.3-6, summarized).

I am not going on to ask, Whom did the prophet have in mind as the sufferer? himself? the Messiah? the people as a whole? a righteous remnant among the people? Nor am I going to ask, Who were those the sufferer suffered for? the people as a whole? the wicked among the people? foreign nations, such as the Babylonians? It is more important for us simply to notice that, over against older ideas, which taught that if you sinned you suffered, so that if you suffered you must have sinned, this new idea began to circulate: perhaps one might suffer, not for his own sins, but for others'; might carry the burden, not of his own guilt, but of others'.

Once this idea came into circulation it stayed in circulation. There was good enough reason why it should. The religion of the Jews became a religion of martyrdom. Before any Christian gave his life for his faith, countless Jews had done so. There was, for example, a dark time in the second century B.C., when Palestine was governed by a Greek king, Antiochus Epiphanes. For reasons of his own – not all of them bad ones – he decided to impose his own religion on the inhabitants of Palestine. In the end they decided to fight for their faith, but before that they simply died for it. Those who were ready to die were, on any showing, those who were most devoted to their faith. Why then, on a religious view of life, should they, precisely they, be the ones to suffer and die? What meaning could be given to their courage and devotion? Again the answer was given: they were suffering not so much for their own sins as for the sins of the people at large, and because they were willing to suffer God would have mercy on his people and deliver them.

By channels such as these Isaiah's thought flowed down into New Testament times. One, if he was good enough, might suffer for the rest, and by his suffering win their freedom. This, said the New Testament writers, or some of them, is exactly what has happened. – Christ 'did no sin, no guile was found in his mouth. When he was reviled he did not revile again. When he suffered, he did not threaten, but committed himself to him who judges righteously. In his own body he bore our sins on the tree, that we, having died to sins, might live for righteousness. By his wounds you were healed. For you were going astray, like sheep; but now you have returned to the Shepherd and Guardian of your souls.'

That quotation is from the first epistle of Peter (2.22-25); it is surprising that the New Testament does not make more use than it does of this great passage. But there may have been good reasons for this. Certainly the New Testament writers did not wish to represent Jesus as just another one in the long line of the army of martyrs. He was more than this. And perhaps the process seemed just a bit too automatic; it can be made to seem so. He was wounded, we are healed; his wound becomes our cure. It is possible to put this in a way that becomes morally intolerable – as if God, being a vindictive sort of person, felt himself injured and under an inner compulsion to punish someone. The real culprits managed to keep out of the way, and Jesus took their place. God was satisfied because he could take it out of someone, and we profited because he took it out of Jesus, and not out of us. I am not saying that any Christian ever believed such a blasphemy as this. But it is possible, if you are not careful, sometimes to make Christian teaching sound like this. What has to be remembered is that God is interested in people, not in paper transactions. He is not content to pretend that Jesus is I, and in that character to punish him; and then to pretend that I am Jesus, and in that character to reward me. He will not be content until I have suffered with Christ, and come to a new life, in which I actually display the goodness Jesus showed in his life and death.

We shall see more and more of this as we continue to study the way in which the New Testament speaks of Christ crucified. For the moment it may suffice to put it like this. The New Testament does say, Christ died for me. But it also says, I have been crucified with Christ. The New Testament does say, Christ is alive, for us. But it also says, I live no longer, Christ lives in me. That is, the New Testament comes to the conclusion that the crucifixion and resurrection of Jesus made up one event, which may be looked at in two ways. It was something that happened outside us, independently of us; and it is something that happens within us, a reproduction of what happened outside. The first of these (what happens outside us) is expressed to perfection by the figure of the sufferer in Isaiah 53, and that is why Christian people will always come back to it and say, All we like sheep have gone astray, and the Lord hath laid on him the iniquity of us all. But the second (what happens within us) is not so clearly brought out by Isaiah, and this perhaps is why the New Testament makes less use of this great chapter of his than we might expect. How can this second truth be expressed? We must go on to look for this.

V. THE SON OF MAN

AFTER THE first Good Friday and Easter the disciples of
Jesus found themselves obliged to explain, as well as they
could, for their own benefit and for the benefit of their contemporaries, events which had evidently taken them by sur-
prise, events for which there was no current explanation
available for them to use. We are noting specimens of the
ways in which they attacked their problem. Their first step
was to recognize that what Jesus had done in his death was
of a piece with what he had been doing all through his life.
His humble life and his ignominious death were, surprisingly,
stages God had chosen to take in the process of setting up
his kingdom. They looked at the religious environment with
which they were familiar, and could not fail to notice that
Jesus had died at Passover time. His last meal with his disciples had been at any rate a kind of Passover meal. Passover
meant the deliverance and purification of God's people:
there was evidently something to work on here, and other
Jewish religious practices could be drawn on too. It was
natural also to look back into the Old Testament, and to
read passages like Isaiah 53, with its picture of the innocent
and righteous Sufferer, with eyes that had been opened by
the actual sufferings of the innocent and righteous Jesus.
There were other Old Testament passages, too, which we
have not had time to look at.

We have not yet noticed what must have been the most
natural step of all – to consider what, if anything, Jesus himself had had to say about his approaching suffering. If we
may judge from the gospels, when he had spoken of it he had
not done so in terms of Jewish feasts, or in terms of the
innocent Sufferer of Isaiah 53, though to do this
seems natural enough to us; he had used a different expression. When he foretold suffering to come, he predicted
it for the Son of man.

He began to teach them that the Son of man must suffer
many things, and be rejected by the elders and the chief
priests and the scribes, and be killed, and after three days

rise up (Mark 8.31).

How is it written of the Son of man, that he should suffer many things and be set at nought? (Mark 9.12).

The Son of man is to be handed over into the power of men, and they shall kill him; and after he has been killed he will after three days rise up (Mark 9.31).

And they were on the way, going up to Jerusalem, and Jesus was going in front of them, and they were amazed, and those who were following were afraid. And again he took the Twelve, and began to tell them the things that were going to happen to him: Look, we are going up to Jerusalem, and the Son of man shall be handed over to the chief priests and the scribes, and they shall condemn him to death and hand him over to the Gentiles, and they shall mock him and spit on him and scourge him and kill him; and after three days he shall rise up (Mark 10.32-34).

The Son of man is going, just as it stands written about him; but woe to that man through whom the Son of man is handed over; it would be a good thing for that man if he had never been born (Mark 14.21).

It is, I think, important that we should notice how the material in the gospels that deals with the suffering of Jesus is focused on this term, Son of man. Before the crucifixion Jesus does not say, The Christ must suffer; or, The Son of God must suffer; or, The Servant of the Lord must suffer. He does say, The Son of man must suffer.

So much for predictions of suffering. There are few passages in the gospels that offer any explanation of why there must be suffering, but here too the title Son of man is used.

Even the Son of man came not to be served but to serve, and to give his life as a ransom for many (Mark 10.45).

As Moses lifted up the snake in the wilderness, so must the Son of man be lifted up, that every one who believes may have eternal life in him (John 3.14,15).

I find it hard to believe that this concentration on 'Son of man' is accidental or insignificant. There must be some special connection between Son of man and suffering, though it is not at first easy to see what this connection is. In the gospels, moreover, the expression 'Son of man' is used in other ways too. It is used, for example, in describing Jesus' earthly life, sometimes in speaking of his authority, and sometimes in speaking of his rejection by those he came to serve.

The Son of man has authority on earth to forgive sins (Mark 2.10).

The Son of man is lord even of the Sabbath (Mark 2.28). In these verses we see the claim that Jesus has an authority greater than the Jewish law: he can, for example, override the Sabbath regulations, and when a man has sinned by rebelling against the law, Jesus can renew his relation with God by forgiveness.

The foxes have earths, the birds of the sky have nests, but the Son of man has nowhere to lay his head (Luke 9.58).

John the Baptist came neither eating bread nor drinking wine, and you say, He has a devil. The Son of man came eating and drinking, and you say, Look! a glutton and a toper, a friend of tax-collectors and sinners (Luke 7.33,34).

These verses point on to those we have already seen, where suffering is explicitly predicted: the Son of man will in the end be completely rejected – already people do not like the company he keeps; he will in the end be killed – already he is less fortunate than a hunted fox.

You will remember, however, that in nearly every case the predictions that the Son of man would suffer wound up with the belief that, after suffering and death, he would rise up. Defeat would be followed by victory, death swallowed up by life. In addition there are other sayings that speak of a different manifestation of the Son of man's glory in a more remote future. One example will be enough.

Then they shall see the Son of man coming in clouds, with great power and glory (Mark 13.26).

The first thing that strikes me about this varied group of sayings, all of which contain the title 'Son of man', is that they form a close parallel to the teaching of Jesus about the kingdom of God, which we briefly looked at in the second talk. At one end of the story the kingdom of God is so small as to be scarcely noticeable, or, if noticed, despised. It is like the small seed, wastefully disposed of in the process of sowing. Nothing (you would suppose) would ever come of that! And

indeed nothing does – unless it dies. At the other end of the
story is the kingdom in glory and power: the huge plant, the
plentiful harvest, the final victory of God over the powers
that resist his will-to-good. Both the sayings about the kingdom of God, and the sayings about the Son of man, reflect
the way in which God chooses to work, and the Son of man
is a crystallization in personal terms of what God does as he
sets up his kingdom. If you believe in God at all, it is easy to
imagine that he could eliminate the forces of evil at once,
destroying them with a single blow. He could, no doubt,
immediately assert his own sovereignty, and claim and exercise all his own rights. Why does he not do this? Because it
would not be like him to do so; because it would not achieve
the end he aims at. He is not that kind of autocrat. He
is patient and long-suffering, and would rather take his creat-
ures with him in willing obedience than stamp them out as the
rebels they undoubtedly are. Unlike human dictators, his
intention is not to create a desolation and call that peace, or
victory. He would rather reconcile the world than destroy it.

This means that God will introduce his kingdom gently,
secretly, giving men the opportunity to understand and
accept it; and, though no doubt other ways of doing this
could be thought of, it is hard to think of a better one than
that of presenting the kingdom to men in the form of a man,
who showed in his own character the virtues of the kingdom,
who could on occasion wield its power, and who made himself known as the one who, in the name of God, offered to
his fellows the forgiveness of their sins, and challenged them
to obedience.

But there is more to say than this. The Son of man means
man. What is man? That is an Old Testament question.

When I consider thy heavens, the work of thy fingers,
The moon and the stars, which thou hast ordained;
What is man that thou art mindful of him?
And the son of man, that thou visitest him?
For thou hast made him but little lower than God,
And crowned him with glory and honour.
Thou madest him to have dominion over the works of thy
    hands;

Thou hast put all things under his feet:
All sheep and oxen,
Yea, and the beasts of the field;
The fowl of the air, and the fish of the sea,
Whatsoever passeth through the paths of the seas
    (Psalm 8.3-8).

Alongside that quotation I should like to put another. The second is not from the Bible, but from *Hamlet*.

What a piece of work is a man! how noble in reason! how infinite in faculty! in form and moving how express and admirable! in action how like an angel! in apprehension how like a god! the beauty of the world! the paragon of animals! And yet, to me, what is this quintessence of dust? man delights not me.

Hamlet is right: there is something wrong with this godlike creature, a cancer in his vitals, a rot that undermines the dominion man should exercise under God over the rest of creation. And we, who see man threatened by the devices he himself has made, should know it better than Hamlet did.

There is only one way for man to regain his sovereignty over creation, the sovereignty he was intended to exercise, and of which vestiges appear all through man's history and in his dealings with the world of nature. This one way is that he should recognize that, great as he is, he is nevertheless lower than God. He only reigns as an intermediate agent between God and the universe. That is, the establishing of God's reign and the vindication of man's place within it are bound up with man's complete obedience to God.

It is here that the story and the teaching of Jesus come together and make one complete intelligible whole. The figure of the Son of man, this being of mingled dignity and abject humiliation, of authority over men, angels, and devils, and of obedience unto death, is man, as he is caught up in the kingdom of God. You cannot separate Jesus the Son of man from the kingdom of God. Nor in the end can you separate their weakness and their power. As soon as you try to put the matter in the form of a story it looks like a tale with a happy ending; but truly the glory and the victory are implicit in the suffering, for it is in the suffering that human obedience, which on the stage of history manifests the reign of God, becomes complete.

Jesus, then, is the man in whom the reign of God is manifested, in whom God's kingdom comes. And this he is not simply on his own account, but for others too.

It is an odd thing that, though Jesus constantly speaks of the Son of man, hardly anyone else in the New Testament does so. Why is this? Mainly, I think, because the phrase seems in Greek a very odd one (as it does, when you come to think of it, in English). But if the New Testament writers, outside the gospels, avoid the phrase, this does not mean that they did not share the idea. We must remember that 'Son of man' means man – perhaps Man, with a capital M. Remembering this, recall the words of Paul:

> Since by man came death, by man came also the resurrection of the dead;
>
> For as in Adam all die, even so in Christ shall all be made alive (1 Corinthians 15.21,22).

By speaking of Adam, Paul calls to mind the story of the man who determined to live in and for himself; to make himself secure in his own enjoyment of life. He had no intention of being even a little lower than God; he meant to be on precisely the same level. By attempting this, he upset the balance of the universe. 'By man came death.' This is true; it does not matter whether you think of the old story of Adam as history or as myth; the upshot is the same. This is the story of man. We all belong to the one human family, and all show the same family characteristics of looking after ourselves, rebelling against God, – and failing, for in the end we all die. As Paul says, we all carry the stamp of Adam upon us. 'Every man kills the thing he loves'; and in the end destroys himself.

It is in Jesus that this process is reversed, for instead of killing what he loved he gave his life for it. Instead of seeking, like Adam, to have life in and for himself, he gave life away in obedience to God; and in his death is our life, for with it there begins the possibility that we may live as he lived, in that obedience which reconstitutes man's dominion, under God's sovereignty.

VI. CONCLUSION

In this last talk let me first of all go right back to the beginning and remind you of what we have been trying to do. At this time of the year our minds picture the crucifixion and resurrection of Jesus. How are we to think of them? First of all, as things that really happened. Most of us have known about them for so long, and have got so used to seeing them in a context of church services and official doctrine, that this takes an effort of the imagination. The effort required is all the greater because we do not possess all the information that, as historians, we should like to have. The story contains many loose ends, and apparent contradictions. The essential points stand out quite clearly: neither Jews nor Romans could tolerate Jesus of Nazareth, and they disposed of him by crucifixion; but after his death those who had known him best, recovered from the consternation and confusion into which his death had thrown them when they became convinced that he was alive again. We do not know precisely the legal processes by which the death of Jesus was engineered, nor do we know what the disciples of Jesus had been expecting. We can see pretty clearly that both the crucifixion and the resurrection caught them off balance. When Jesus was alive they had not expected him to be killed – at any rate, not in this way; and when he was dead they had not expected him to come to life. And unlike the modern theologian they were not provided with a score of fat text books, all ready to explain to them the doctrine of the atonement, and why it was right for Jesus to save men from their sins by dying a bloody death.

This meant that they had to think. They explored the resources of the religion in which they had been brought up: they re-read the Old Testament; they searched their memories, and tried to remember, and to see in the new light which now shone round them, what Jesus himself had taught. We have tried, in what could only be a rather scrappy way, to follow them in their quest. Having asked first, What happened? we went on with the question, How did people

35

react to it? How did they explain it to themselves and to others?

This has called for hard digging; I hope you have not given up; I hope you will find it worth-while in the end. I think you will have seen at least glimpses of journey's end as we have trudged along a sometimes dusty road. Take this, first. What do you make of life? your own life? the life of the human family as a whole? What is the purpose of existence, as it drags on, day after day, age after age? Some people say there is no purpose. It just drags on, and that is all there is to say. Others will say, If there is a purpose, there is no means of knowing what it is; we live in the dark. The New Testament answer to this comes in two stages. There is a purpose in life, a purpose that will be plain enough when the story has reached its end; what is more, the end has already appeared in the middle of the story. The death and resurrection of Jesus show the meaning God puts on life, and manifest the pattern of history as God himself understands it. They sound the theme on which the whole of history is a set of variations of unbelievable complexity and range. Like any good composer, God always has surprises, new modulations and inversions, up his sleeve, so that no one can give a full explanation of any single human life, still less of the whole sweep of history. But if you look at Christ, crucified and risen, you will see the whole theme played through in its simplest form and to the final cadence. You do not need to wait till the end of time; you can see the meaning here.

After this, we spoke of the Passover – and this could easily seem a waste of time. What have we to do with the Passover? The Passover is about God; it tells you what sort of God he is. It reminds you that he is not content to leave men in their bondage, that he means to put down the mighty from their seats, and exalt the humble and poor. God acts in faithful love on behalf of the needy. The Old Testament story itself tells you this; the story of Jesus tells it still more plainly. Passover may seem an unpromising beginning for a line of thought, but when you see it in the light of the crucifixion it proclaims the very core of the good news: God is faithful,

God loves, God saves.

Then you can ask another question: Why do men suffer? Why do good men suffer? There is no question that so erodes our faith as this one. There are, I know, some who say, Because of what I have learned of modern scientific thought I no longer believe in the existence of God; but I suspect that for every one such person you could find a hundred who would say, Because of what I have seen of human suffering I no longer believe in the love of God – and therefore do not care whether he exists or not. But if it is true not merely that God could use the innocent suffering of some obscure character in the Old Testament, but chose himself to adopt suffering as his way of loving, then we can begin to see our way through that problem.

If, as I believe, there is relevance for us in the three points I have just mentioned, then we are home, for as soon as we reach Jesus' own description of himself as the Son of man – the Man who lives, suffers, dies, and triumphs – we have certainly caught up with ourselves. This is the picture of man as God designed him, reigning in the universe with God alone as his superior; and the resurrection means that God is not going to be beaten in his purpose.

This brings us to the last question we can attempt to clear up in these talks. I think we have now got as far as this. We have followed the first Christians, whose ideas are reflected in the New Testament, as they wrestled with the events they had witnessed and taken part in, and tried to make rational and communicable sense of what these events had meant to them. We have looked at some of the images and thoughts they used. We have seen that, even when they used images and thoughts that would not have suggested themselves to us, they were nevertheless talking about real things, which we can recognize as real because they belong to our experience too. But we may none the less be left with the question in our minds, How can things that happened so long ago affect me now? About this, there are three things to say. They are all important; and it is important to keep all of them in mind and in proportion. From time to time Christians have left one out, or have over-emphasized one at the expense of the other two; whenever this has happened their Christianity has been left unbalanced and distorted.

The first is this. We are dealing, as I have said, with things that happened; yesterday and tomorrow – Good Friday and Easter Day – we begin by reading pages out of the history book. It is an extraordinary thing that we possess gospels in which to read these records. To Christians in the first century, Jesus Christ was the Lord who reigned in heaven at the right hand of God. There he was making intercession for them; thence he had sent his Spirit to guide and empower them. Why should they write books about the obscure carpenter, Jesus of Nazareth? They would have answered, We have no choice in the matter. This is where it all began; we did not invent a new religion. The Lord in heaven is a meaningless idea unless he is the person we have seen and heard and known. That he lives is nothing, unless he died; and that he died is nothing, unless he was the man who lived and spoke as no one else ever lived and spoke. The whole story of redemption gets its moral content and significance from what men remembered and believed about Jesus of Nazareth, seen in the light of the Old Testament revelation, which he summed up and carried to a greater height. A religion, therefore, that cannot find room for such simple statements as 'He went about doing good', and 'He came not to be served but to serve', is simply not the religion of the New Testament; it may be airy mysticism, it may be dry-as-dust theology, but it is not Christianity. On the other hand, a religion that finds room for nothing else but these will become mere 'do-goodism', or a cheerful bonhomie that the world can produce as well as the church.

We must therefore begin with the story of the man who lived and died in Palestine, who was as real a man as we ourselves. If this were not true we should have no gospels to read. As we read them, however, and especially as we go on to read the rest of the New Testament, we meet the conviction that behind this man, visible in his acts and audible in his words, is God. This is the second of the three things that must be said. What you say about Jesus, you can, with

only a little modification, say about God. To take at once
the most important of examples, you can say of Jesus, He
loved me and gave himself up for me (Galatians 2.20); you
can also say of God, that he so loved the world that he gave
his only Son (John 3.16). The story of Jesus is the truth
about God. There is no other description of God that really
matters; nor is there any other account of Jesus that really
makes sense. There are, I understand, some people who
would like to get rid of God, and keep only Jesus. If they
mean to do this they will have to find a different Jesus from
the one who appears in the gospels. In one way and another
he constantly repeats that he is not acting on his own account.
He is there because he has been sent. He has no purpose in
life but to be obedient – obedient to what? To nothing? To
a dead God? If God is dead, or if he never existed, then
Jesus was a fool, and we had better give him up along with
his Father. But if Jesus was right, we know God; not in the
depth of his being, which we shall never plumb, but in all
that we need to know of him.

There is more to say about this. Jesus did not speculate
about God; he acted in his name. If Jesus reveals God, he
reveals a God who acts. The crucifixion and resurrection,
therefore, the climax of Jesus' life, mean God in action. In
the total event of Jesus Christ God did something for the
human race. What did he do? And how does it affect us?
At this point we can only use analogies, and all the analogies
break down. He won a victory. Over what? Over the devil.
But what is the devil to me, except as I meet him in my own
heart, and – for me – what victory and what defeat can
matter except the victories won and the defeats suffered
there? He offered sacrifice. To whom? To himself? Does
any sacrifice avail for me, until I offer myself to God, and
for my fellowmen? The analogies break down – of course,
for we are talking, or trying to talk, about God, and this is
like trying to put a powerful current through a thin piece of
fuse wire. But the analogies are not meaningless – again,
because we are speaking about God. It is because things
happened in Palestine, and because God was in them, that
victory and sacrifice become possible for me, and I must

never say either, God has left me to look after myself, or, God has done everything, and what I do does not matter.

This leads to the last of the three points. What Jesus did, he did as the Son of man, the representative Man, who acts on behalf of all mankind, and in our place. Whatever this representativeness may mean, it does not mean that since the time of Jesus all men must automatically live like him. By his crucifixion and resurrection he has created a new possibility for the human race; he has opened a new world. But the new possibility consists precisely in this, that his crucifixion and resurrection are reproduced in me. What is the Cross to me but a minor black spot on the history of the Roman Empire, unless with Paul I can say, I have been crucified with Christ? (Galatians 2.19). And what is the resurrection but an antique fable, unless I can add, The life I now live in the flesh, I live by faith in the Son of God? (Galatians 2.20). And these things I may learn to say when, having surveyed the Cross with all the emotion that it properly evokes, I have moved beyond the shame and the ebullience of adolescent Christian feeling into life in which self is daily crucified in the service of my fellows, life which derives its meaning from God, and finds its goal in him.